On Your Plate

Fruit
Honor Head

A⁺
Smart Apple Media

Smart Apple Media
P.O. Box 3263, Mankato, Minnesota 56002

Printed in the United States

Published by arrangement with the Watts Publishing Group Ltd, London.

Created by Taglines
Design: Sumit Charles; Harleen Mehta, Q2A Media
Picture research: Pritika Ghura, Q2A Media

Picture credits
t=top b=bottom c=center l=left r=right m= middle

Cover Images: Shutterstock
Carole Gomez/ Shutterstock: 6tl, Hugo Chang: 6b, Elena Kalistratova/ Shutterstock: 7b, Ljupco Smokovski/
Shutterstock: 8tl, ann triling/ Shutterstock: 8bl, Olga Lyubkina/ Shutterstock: 8br, Photononstop/ Photolibrary: 9b,
Simon Krzic/ Shutterstock: 10, Tina Rencelj/ Istockphoto: 11bl, Lim Yong Hian/ Shutterstock: 11br, Paul Bodea/
Shutterstock: 12bl, SERDAR YAGCI/ Shutterstock: 12br, Tomas Bogner/ Shutterstock: 13b, Chris Bence/ Shutterstock: 14l,
Yuriy Korchagin/ Shutterstock: 14r, Shanta Giddens/ Shutterstock: 15, Rade Lukovic/ Shutterstock: 16, Gene_l |
Dreamstime.com: 17, David Kay/ Shutterstock: 18, Rognar | Dreamstime.com: 19, Tray Berry/ Istockphoto: 20,
Jose Manuel Gelpi Diaz/ Shutterstock: 21.

Library of Congress Cataloging-in-Publication Data

Head, Honor.
  Fruit / Honor Head.
      p. cm. -- (On your plate)
  Includes index.
  Summary: "Provides a basic introduction to common fruits and explains how they are grown,
  different ways to eat them, and how they keep you healthy."--Provided by publisher.
  ISBN 978-1-59920-260-0 (hardcover)
  1. Cookery (Fruit)--Juvenile literature. 2. Fruit--Juvenile literature. I. Title.
  TX811.H43 2010
  641.3'4--dc22
                                                            2008038768

9 8 7 6 5 4 3 2 1

Contents

What is fruit?

Fruit is a type of food that grows on trees, bushes, and vines.

Apples grow on trees.

All fruits have seeds or pits.
New plants grow from these.

The middle of the
apple is called
the core. This is
where the seeds are.

seed

Oranges

orange

mandarin orange

Oranges are citrus fruit. Citrus fruits have a thick skin called peel.

slice

peel

tangerine

 Tangerines are smaller than most oranges.

The vitamin C found in oranges keeps you from getting a cold.

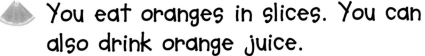 You eat oranges in slices. You can also drink orange juice.

Melons

watermelon

Melons are sweet and juicy.
You can eat them sliced.

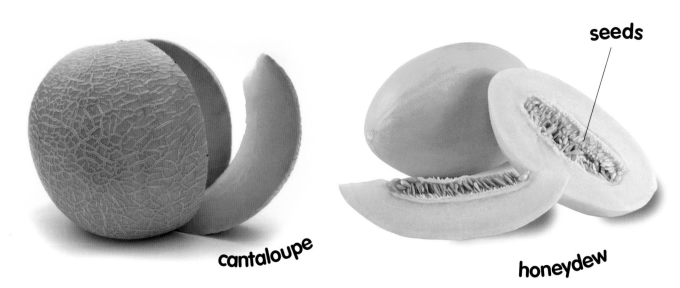

seeds

cantaloupe

honeydew

 There are lots of different types of melon.

All melons have seeds inside.
You must be careful not to
eat the seeds.

Melons are
delicious on a hot
summer's day.

9

Pears

Pears grow on trees. They hang down by their brown stems.

These ripe pears are ready to pick.

Most pears are soft and sweet. Some pears are hard.

seeds

Pears have small seeds in the middle.

Pineapples

Pineapples have
spiky green leaves
on top.

Pineapples are
very juicy.

A pineapple has a rough, brown skin. You must cut off the skin before you eat the fruit.

You can cut a pineapple into slices or cubes.

Bananas

Bananas grow in bunches.
When they are growing,
they are green.

green bananas just picked

ripe bananas

Ripe bananas have
bright yellow skin.

14

To eat a banana, just peel back the skin.

Have a banana for a quick and filling snack.

15

Peaches

Peaches have a soft, fuzzy skin that you can eat.

pit

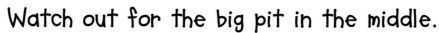 Watch out for the big pit in the middle.

You can buy sliced, skinned peaches in a can. They taste smooth and sweet.

Try canned peaches with your oatmeal.

Grapes

You can buy grapes in big or small bunches.

 Grapes grow on a plant called a vine.

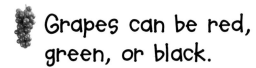 Grapes can be red, green, or black.

Some grapes have little seeds in the middle. Try not to swallow the seeds.

Strawberries

Strawberries are soft and sweet. Their seeds grow on the outside.

You can eat the whole strawberry except the leaves.

Strawberries are eaten mostly in the summer.

Strawberries are good to eat on their own, or with ice cream.

Things to Do

Which one?

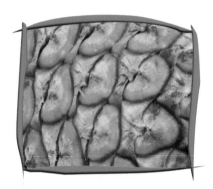 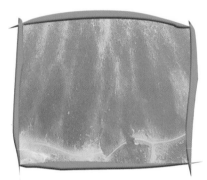 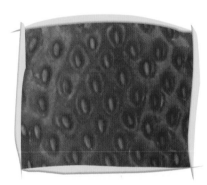

Which of these fruits is a strawberry? Which is an orange? What is the other fruit?

Guess it!

You can play this game with a friend or in a group.

Begin by saying, "My favorite fruit is_____". Then say what it looks like and how it tastes. Be sure not to say its name!

The first person to guess the name of your fruit has the next turn.

Fruit Puzzle

How many different fruits can you see in this puzzle?
Can you name them all?

Glossary

bushes
A large plant with many branches.

citrus fruit
Fruits that have a skin called peel

ripe
When a food is ready to be picked

skinned
Fruit that has had all its skin taken off

vitamin C
Something the body needs to stay healthy

Index